A Special Gift

Presented to:

_____

From:

_____

Date:

_____

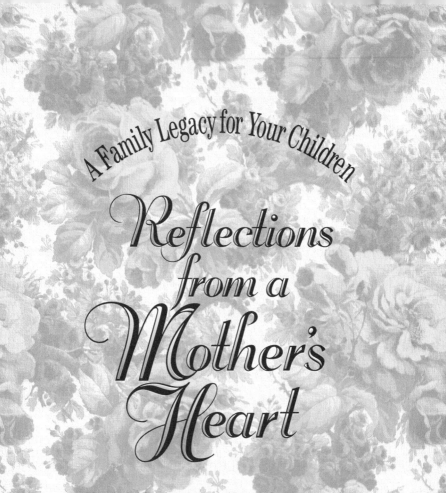

A Family Legacy for Your Children

Reflections
from a
Mother's
Heart

Your Life Story in Your Own Words

WORD PUBLISHING

Dallas · London · Vancouver · Melbourne

J. Countryman is a registered trademark
of Word Publishing, Inc.

A J. Countryman Book

Designed by Koechel Peterson Design, Inc.,
Minneapolis, Minnesota

Edited by Terri Gibbs

ISBN: 0-8499-5215-8

Printed and bound in the United States of America

789 RRD 9

Contents

Introduction

*D*ays pass…seasons change…months meld into years, and we stand looking back at our lives—childhood memories, exciting moments, crises, and turning points.

In January we think of new beginnings; in February of valentines, first dates, and first kisses. Does ever a June pass without thoughts of our own wedding day? Surely summer evokes backseat memories of seemingly unending trips to grandma's house or the beach. And don't November and December bring to mind family traditions and celebrations held tightly through the years?

Like ivy on the garden trellis, our lives are inescapably entwined with the seasons and months of the year. That is why we have designed this mother's memory journal in a twelve-month format. Each month features twelve intriguing questions with space to write a personal answer. Questions explore family history, childhood memories, lighthearted incidents, cherished traditions, and the dreams and spiritual adventures encountered in a lifetime of living.

Whether you choose to complete the journal in a few days, weeks, or over the course of a year, the questions will take you on a journey through the times and seasons of your life. This makes a tangible family record to pass on as a gift to a son or daughter, a loving memoir of written words that are windows to a mother's heart.

No matter what your age, memory and reminiscence open a richer, fuller understanding of who you are as a family. Let this memory journal be a starting point—a door into discussing and sharing the unique qualities of your life. May *Reflections from a Mother's Heart* draw you closer to each other as you share the experiences of a lifetime. &

Personal Portrait

your full given name _____.

your date of birth _____.

your place of birth _____.

your mother's full name _____.

   the place and date of her birth _____.

your father's full name _____.

   the place and date of his birth _____.

the names of your paternal grandparents _____.

   the places and dates of their births _____.

the names of your maternal grandparents _____.

   the places and dates of their births _____.

the names of your siblings _____.

   the places and dates of their births _____.

   _____.

   _____.

the date and place of your marriage _____.

the full given name of your husband _____.

the names and birth dates of your children _____.

   _____.

   _____.

What is your favorite?

flower _____.   Bible verse _____.

perfume _____.   dessert _____.

color _____.   vacation spot _____.

hymn or song _____.   type of food _____.

book _____.   sport _____.

author _____.   leisure activity _____.

9

JANUARY

*T*he beauty of

the written word is that

it can be held

close to the heart and read

over and over again.

FLORENCE LITTAUER

What was your favorite pastime as a child? Did you prefer doing it alone or with someone else? _____.

Who gave you your name and why? Did you have a family nickname? How did you get it? _____.

_____
_____
_____
_____
_____
_____
_____
_____
_____
_____
_____
_____
_____
_____
_____
_____
_____
_____
_____
_____
_____
_____
_____

*D*escribe your childhood bedroom. What was the view from your window? _____.

_____
_____
_____
_____
_____
_____
_____
_____
_____
_____
_____
_____
_____
_____
_____
_____
_____
_____
_____
_____
_____
_____
_____

Were you baptized or dedicated as an infant? If so, where and by whom?

_____

_____.

_____.

_____.

_____.

_____.

_____.

_____.

_____.

_____.

_____.

_____.

_____.

_____.

_____.

_____.

_____.

_____.

_____.

_____.

_____.

_____.

_____.

_____.

When did you first go to church? What are your earliest memories of church?

*W*here did your father go to work every day and what did he do? _____.

_____
_____
_____
_____
_____
_____
_____
_____
_____
_____
_____
_____
_____
_____
_____
_____
_____
_____
_____
_____
_____
_____
_____

How did your mother spend her day? Did she have a job or do volunteer work outside the home? _____.

Describe what the family living room looked like when you were a child.

_____.

_____.

_____.

_____.

_____.

_____.

_____.

_____.

_____.

_____.

_____.

_____.

_____.

_____.

_____.

_____.

_____.

_____.

_____.

_____.

_____.

_____.

*W*hat kind of prayer did you say before you went to sleep? Who taught you how to pray it? ———————————.

_____

_____

_____

_____

_____

_____

_____

_____

_____

_____

_____

_____

_____

_____

_____

_____

_____

_____

_____

_____

_____

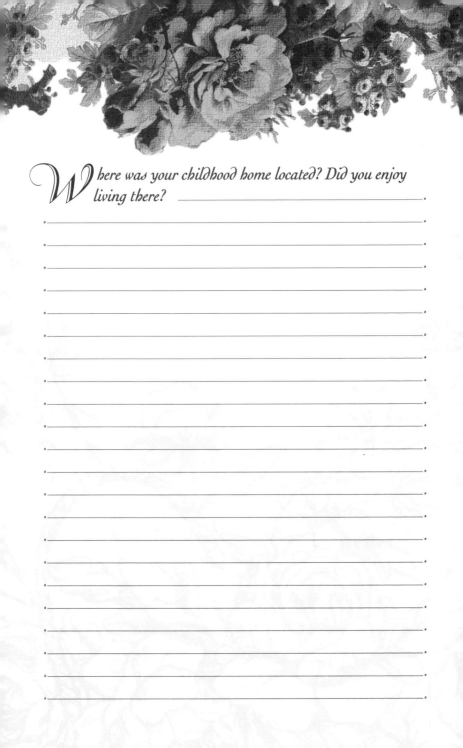

*W*here was your childhood home located? Did you enjoy living there? _____.

_____
_____
_____
_____
_____
_____
_____
_____
_____
_____
_____
_____
_____
_____
_____
_____
_____
_____
_____
_____
_____
_____

Describe your grandparents' houses. Did you visit them often? Why or why not? _____.

_____

_____

_____

_____

_____

_____

_____

_____

_____

_____

_____

_____

_____

_____

_____

_____

_____

_____

_____

_____

_____

_____

List one special memory about each of your brothers and sisters.

———————————————————— •

———————————————————— •

———————————————————— •

• ————————————————————— •

• ————————————————————— •

• ————————————————————— •

• ————————————————————— •

• ————————————————————— •

• ————————————————————— •

• ————————————————————— •

• ————————————————————— •

• ————————————————————— •

• ————————————————————— •

• ————————————————————— •

• ————————————————————— •

• ————————————————————— •

• ————————————————————— •

• ————————————————————— •

• ————————————————————— •

• ————————————————————— •

• ————————————————————— •

January

Recall for me some of the most important lessons you have learned in life:

. _____ .
. _____ .
. _____ .
. _____ .
. _____ .
. _____ .
. _____ .
. _____ .
. _____ .
. _____ .
. _____ .
. _____ .
. _____ .
. _____ .
. _____ .
. _____ .
. _____ .
. _____ .
. _____ .
. _____ .

FEBRUARY

*F*or all of us,
today's experiences are
tomorrow's memories.

BARBARA JOHNSON

Share a memory of your grandparents or an older person you loved. _____.

_____
_____
_____
_____
_____
_____
_____
_____
_____
_____
_____
_____
_____
_____
_____
_____
_____
_____
_____
_____
_____
_____
_____

*W*ho was the first person to talk to you about God? What effect did this have on you? _____.

When did you become a Christian? How did your life change? _____.

_____
_____
_____
_____
_____
_____
_____
_____
_____
_____
_____
_____
_____
_____
_____
_____
_____
_____
_____
_____
_____
_____

Who gave you your first Bible and how old were you when you received it? How did it influence your life?

_____.
_____.
_____.
_____.
_____.
_____.
_____.
_____.
_____.
_____.
_____.
_____.
_____.
_____.
_____.
_____.
_____.
_____.
_____.
_____.

Describe a memorable Valentine you received.

How far did you have to travel to attend elementary, junior high, and high school, and how did you get there? _____.

_____
_____
_____
_____
_____
_____
_____
_____
_____
_____
_____
_____
_____
_____
_____
_____
_____
_____
_____
_____
_____
_____

February

What scent or sound immediately takes you back to childhood? Describe the feeling it evokes. —————.

What was your favorite meal when you were a child? What made it your favorite?

_____.
_____.
_____.
_____.
_____.
_____.
_____.
_____.
_____.
_____.
_____.
_____.
_____.
_____.
_____.
_____.
_____.
_____.
_____.
_____.
_____.
_____.
_____.
_____.

February

What was the name of your favorite pet? Why was it your favorite?

_____

_____

_____

_____

_____

_____

_____

_____

_____

_____

_____

_____

_____

_____

_____

_____

_____

_____

_____

_____

_____

February

*W*hat chores did you have to do when you were growing up?
Did you get an allowance? How much was it? _____.

_____
_____
_____
_____
_____
_____
_____
_____
_____
_____
_____
_____
_____
_____
_____
_____
_____
_____
_____
_____
_____

February

Tell me about your first job.

*Share a story about a
severe winter storm.*

_____.
_____.
_____.
_____.
_____.
_____.
_____.
_____.
_____.
_____.
_____.
_____.
_____.
_____.
_____.
_____.
_____.
_____.
_____.
_____.
_____.
_____.
_____.
_____.
_____.

Share your favorite dessert recipe:

_____
_____
_____
_____
_____
_____
_____
_____
_____
_____
_____
_____
_____
_____
_____
_____
_____
_____
_____

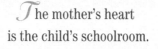

MARCH

*T*he mother's heart
is the child's schoolroom.

HENRY WARD BEECHER

*D*id the pastor or a visiting missionary ever come to your house for dinner or tea? Share one vivid experience. _____.

Did you ever feel that God had a special calling on your life?

When did you first start to pray? What do you remember about your early prayers? ——————————————.

———————————————————————
———————————————————————
———————————————————————
———————————————————————
———————————————————————
———————————————————————
———————————————————————
———————————————————————
———————————————————————
———————————————————————
———————————————————————
———————————————————————
———————————————————————
———————————————————————
———————————————————————
———————————————————————
———————————————————————
———————————————————————
———————————————————————
———————————————————————
———————————————————————
———————————————————————
———————————————————————
———————————————————————

March

Who was your favorite teacher? Why?

_____.
_____.
_____.
_____.
_____.
_____.
_____.
_____.
_____.
_____.
_____.
_____.
_____.
_____.
_____.
_____.
_____.
_____.
_____.
_____.
_____.
_____.
_____.

March

Describe one of your favorite dress-up outfits as a child. On what occasions would you wear it? _____.

_____
_____
_____
_____
_____
_____
_____
_____
_____
_____
_____
_____
_____
_____
_____
_____
_____
_____
_____
_____
_____
_____

$\mathcal{D}$id you ever have a special hideaway or playhouse? What made it special? _____.

What extracurricular activities were you involved in during high school? Why did you choose those activities? _____.

What was the hardest thing you ever had to do?

_____

_____

_____

_____

_____

_____

_____

_____

_____

_____

_____

_____

_____

_____

_____

_____

_____

_____

_____

_____

_____

_____

_____

_____

March

What crazy fads do you remember in grade school? _____.

_____
_____
_____
_____
_____
_____
_____
_____
_____
_____
_____
_____
_____
_____
_____
_____
_____
_____
_____
_____
_____
_____
_____

When did you have your first date? Tell me about it.

_____
_____
_____
_____
_____
_____
_____
_____
_____
_____
_____
_____
_____
_____
_____
_____
_____
_____
_____
_____
_____
_____

March

What do you remember about your first kiss? _____.

What did you do to celebrate birthdays when you were growing up?

_____

_____

_____

_____

_____

_____

_____

_____

_____

_____

_____

_____

_____

_____

_____

_____

_____

_____

_____

_____

_____

March

Record here some gardening or decorating tips that you have found helpful:

_____

_____

_____

_____

_____

_____

_____

_____

_____

_____

_____

_____

_____

_____

_____

_____

_____

_____

_____

APRIL

However time or circumstance
may come between
a mother and her child,
their lives are
interwoven forever.

PAM BROWN

What were some of the most memorable books you read as a child? What made them memorable? _____.

_____
_____
_____
_____
_____
_____
_____
_____
_____
_____
_____
_____
_____
_____
_____
_____
_____
_____
_____
_____
_____
_____
_____

What were your family finances like when you were growing up? How did that affect you?

_____

_____
_____
_____
_____
_____
_____
_____
_____
_____
_____
_____
_____
_____
_____
_____
_____
_____
_____
_____
_____
_____
_____

April

*D*o you remember your first communion? What influence did it have on you and your family? _____.

What mischievous childhood experience do you remember? How did it affect you?

_____

_____

_____

_____

_____

_____

_____

_____

_____

_____

_____

_____

_____

_____

_____

_____

_____

_____

_____

_____

_____

_____

_____

What meaningful advice did you receive from an adult?
What were the circumstances? _____.

_____
_____
_____
_____
_____
_____
_____
_____
_____
_____
_____
_____
_____
_____
_____
_____
_____
_____
_____
_____
_____
_____
_____

As a teenager did you rebel or do things your parents wouldn't have approved of? How do you feel about that now? _____.

April

When did you first learn about sex? What was your reaction?

What things do you wish you had done in childhood or adolescence?

_____.
_____.
_____.
_____.
_____.
_____.
_____.
_____.
_____.
_____.
_____.
_____.
_____.
_____.
_____.
_____.
_____.
_____.
_____.
_____.
_____.
_____.
_____.
_____.

What are the things you are most glad you tried? _____.

*D*escribe your mother in her best dress. _____.

April

Describe your father in his working clothes. _____.

What did your family like to do on weekends? Describe one particularly memorable event.

_____.

_____.

_____.

_____.

_____.

_____.

_____.

_____.

_____.

_____.

_____.

_____.

_____.

_____.

_____.

_____.

_____.

_____.

_____.

_____.

_____.

_____.

_____.

Share one of your mother's best recipes or a recipe for one of your favorite childhood dishes:

_____

_____

_____

_____

_____

_____

_____

_____

_____

_____

_____

_____

_____

_____

_____

_____

_____

_____

_____

MAY

*I*n search of
my mother's garden,
I found my own.

ALICE WALKER

What toys did you like to play with? Why those particular toys? _____

_____

_____

_____

_____

_____

_____

_____

_____

_____

_____

_____

_____

_____

_____

_____

_____

_____

_____

_____

_____

_____

_____

_____

How old were you when you understood that God loves you? Recall your early thoughts about God's love. —————.

———————————————————
———————————————————
———————————————————
———————————————————
———————————————————
———————————————————
———————————————————
———————————————————
———————————————————
———————————————————
———————————————————
———————————————————
———————————————————
———————————————————
———————————————————
———————————————————
———————————————————
———————————————————
———————————————————
———————————————————
———————————————————

May

Describe a time in your life when you feel God led you in an unusual way.

Did you ever go to a dance?
Tell me about it.

——————————————.
——————————————.
——————————————.
————————————————————.
————————————————————.
————————————————————.
————————————————————.
————————————————————.
————————————————————.
————————————————————.
————————————————————.
————————————————————.
————————————————————.
————————————————————.
————————————————————.
————————————————————.
————————————————————.
————————————————————.
————————————————————.
————————————————————.
————————————————————.

May

What kind of car did your family drive? Were you proud of it or embarrassed by it? Why? _____.

_____
_____
_____
_____
_____
_____
_____
_____
_____
_____
_____
_____
_____
_____
_____
_____
_____
_____
_____
_____
_____
_____
_____
_____
_____

Did you attend family reunions? Share a memory of one.

May

Did you go to church or community potlucks? How were they important to you and your family?

Tell about someone who influenced your life profoundly.

*W*here did you go to grade school? Junior High? High School? Tell me about your best childhood friend. _____.

If you went to college or to a career training school, where did you go and why? _____

_____
_____
_____
_____
_____
_____
_____
_____
_____
_____
_____
_____
_____
_____
_____
_____
_____
_____
_____
_____
_____

May

*W*here did you live when you were going to college or developing a career? Describe an unforgettable experience from that time in your life. _____.

_____
_____
_____
_____
_____
_____
_____
_____
_____
_____
_____
_____
_____
_____
_____
_____
_____
_____
_____
_____
_____
_____
_____

What were your youthful goals and ambitions for life? Which ones have you been able to fulfill?

_____.
_____.
_____.
_____.
_____.
_____.
_____.
_____.
_____.
_____.
_____.
_____.
_____.
_____.
_____.
_____.
_____.
_____.
_____.
_____.
_____.
_____.

May

Share some insights from Scripture that have guided your spiritual journey:

_____

_____

_____

_____

_____

_____

_____

_____

_____

_____

_____

_____

_____

_____

_____

_____

_____

_____

_____

JUNE

*R*ings and jewels

are not gifts,

but apologies for gifts.

The only gift

is a portion of thyself.

RALPH WALDO EMERSON

If you learned to play a musical instrument, tell me your memories of lessons, practice, and your music teacher. If not, what instrument did you want to play and why? _____.

*W*hat fashions were popular when you were in high school? Did you like them? Why or why not? _____.

_____
_____
_____
_____
_____
_____
_____
_____
_____
_____
_____
_____
_____
_____
_____
_____
_____
_____
_____
_____
_____
_____
_____
_____

June

How old were you when you met Dad and what attracted you to him?

*When did you first know
you wanted to marry him?
What made you feel that way?*

_____.

_____.

_____.

_____.

_____.

_____.

_____.

_____.

_____.

_____.

_____.

_____.

_____.

_____.

_____.

_____.

_____.

_____.

_____.

_____.

_____.

_____.

_____.

*S*hare a memory about the way he proposed to you. _____

_____.

._____.

._____.

._____.

_____.

._____.

._____.

._____.

._____.

._____.

._____.

._____.

._____.

._____.

._____.

._____.

._____.

._____.

._____.

._____.

._____.

._____

._____

._____

._____

What did you wear on your wedding day?

*T*ell me about your wedding day, from beginning to end. ___

_____

_____

_____

_____

_____

_____

_____

_____

_____

_____

_____

_____

_____

_____

_____

_____

_____

_____

_____

_____

_____

_____

_____

Did your wedding ceremony include a special vow to each other? What was the significance of it?

_____
_____
_____
_____
_____
_____
_____
_____
_____
_____
_____
_____
_____
_____
_____
_____
_____
_____
_____
_____
_____
_____

June

*W*here did you go on your honeymoon? Share one humorous incident. _____

_____
_____
_____
_____
_____
_____
_____
_____
_____
_____
_____
_____
_____
_____
_____
_____
_____
_____
_____
_____
_____
_____

What was your first house or apartment together like?

*D*o you remember one of the meals you fixed after you were married? How has your cooking changed since then? _____.

What do you love best about Dad now?

_____.

_____.

_____.

_____.

_____.

_____.

_____.

_____.

_____.

_____.

_____.

_____.

_____.

_____.

_____.

_____.

_____.

_____.

_____.

_____.

_____.

_____.

_____.

_____.

Record here some travel tips or suggestions for a fun-filled vacation:

_____
_____
_____
_____
_____
_____
_____
_____
_____
_____
_____
_____
_____
_____
_____
_____
_____
_____
_____

JULY

I look back and see how
I've become who I am by a family
that found sweetness and joy
somewhere inside when . . .
life experience tasted bitter.

KATHY BOICE

$\mathcal{S}$hare a family tradition or memory from the Fourth of July.

Have you ever participated in a rally or demonstration? What was the cause? What were your feelings about it? _____.

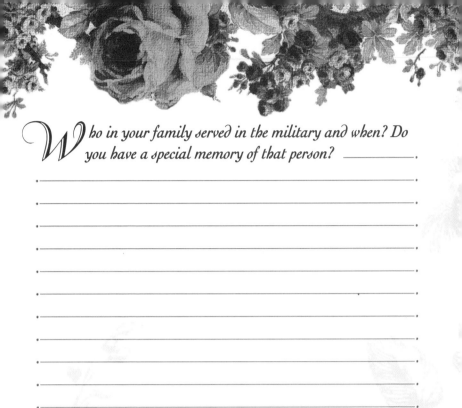

Who in your family served in the military and when? Do you have a special memory of that person? _____.

_____

_____

_____

_____

_____

_____

_____

_____

_____

_____

_____

_____

_____

_____

_____

_____

_____

_____

_____

_____

Did you learn to swim?
How?

————————————.
————————————.
————————————.

July

Did you ever go camping with your family? Where? Record one exceptional camping experience. ——————————.

——————————————————————————————
——————————————————————————————
——————————————————————————————
——————————————————————————————
——————————————————————————————
——————————————————————————————
——————————————————————————————
——————————————————————————————
——————————————————————————————
——————————————————————————————
——————————————————————————————
——————————————————————————————
——————————————————————————————
——————————————————————————————
——————————————————————————————
——————————————————————————————
——————————————————————————————
——————————————————————————————
——————————————————————————————
——————————————————————————————
——————————————————————————————
——————————————————————————————

Tell about your most memorable trip by plane, train, or ship.

Did you ever travel abroad? How old were you and where did you go? Did you travel alone or with a group? _____.

_____
_____
_____
_____
_____
_____
_____
_____
_____
_____
_____
_____
_____
_____
_____
_____
_____
_____
_____
_____
_____
_____

Describe the most fascinating place you have visited.

_____.
_____.
_____.
_____.
_____.
_____.
_____.
_____.
_____.
_____.
_____.
_____.
_____.
_____.
_____.
_____.
_____.
_____.
_____.
_____.
_____.
_____.

Tell about a driving trip with your family. _____

_____

_____

_____

_____

_____

_____

_____

_____

_____

_____

_____

_____

_____

_____

_____

_____

_____

_____

_____

_____

_____

_____

Did your relatives come to visit in the summer or did you go to visit them? What are your memories of those visits. ____.

_____

_____

_____

_____

_____

_____

_____

_____

_____

_____

_____

_____

_____

_____

_____

_____

_____

_____

_____

July

How did you learn to drive? What was your first car like?

Did a tragedy ever strike your family? How were you affected?

_____.

_____.

_____.

July

Share a favorite poem or a passage of writing that has been especially meaningful in your life:

AUGUST

*T*he family—that dear
octopus from whose tentacles
we never quite escape,
nor, in our inmost hearts,
ever quite wish to.

DODIE SMITH

Name a book or author that helped you develop a philosophy of life. Share some of those insights. _____.

_____
_____
_____
_____
_____
_____
_____
_____
_____
_____
_____
_____
_____
_____
_____
_____
_____
_____
_____
_____
_____
_____

*D*id you have a collection when you were growing up? What initially sparked your interest in it? _____.

_____
_____
_____
_____
_____
_____
_____
_____
_____
_____
_____
_____
_____
_____
_____
_____
_____
_____
_____
_____
_____
_____
_____

August

Describe a perfect summer day.

What kind of outdoor work do you like? Hate? Why?

If you could be a patron of a charity or organization, which one would you choose? Why? _____

_____

_____

_____

_____

_____

_____

_____

_____

_____

_____

_____

_____

_____

_____

_____

_____

_____

_____

_____

_____

_____

_____

_____

When did you learn how to ride a bike, or to water ski, snow ski, roller skate, or sail? Share your memories of the experience.

August

What summer games and activities did your family enjoy?

_____

_____

_____

_____

_____

_____

_____

_____

_____

_____

_____

_____

_____

_____

_____

_____

_____

_____

_____

_____

_____

_____

_____

_____

Did you ever milk a cow or spend time on a farm or in the country? Tell me about it.

_____.

_____.

_____.

_____.

_____.

_____.

_____.

_____.

_____.

_____.

_____.

_____.

_____.

_____.

_____.

_____.

_____.

_____.

_____.

_____.

_____.

_____.

_____.

August

Describe your first trip alone.

What places would you still like to visit? Why?

August

Describe a frightening or difficult experience from childhood. How did you respond to it? _____.

_____
_____
_____
_____
_____
_____
_____
_____
_____
_____
_____
_____
_____
_____
_____
_____
_____
_____
_____
_____
_____
_____
_____
_____

*Tell me about your
most unforgettable summer
experience as a child.*

_____.
_____.
_____.
_____.
_____.
_____.
_____.
_____.
_____.
_____.
_____.
_____.
_____.
_____.
_____.
_____.
_____.
_____.
_____.
_____.
_____.
_____.

August

Share some of your ideas about successful entertaining:

_____

_____

_____

_____

_____

_____

_____

_____

_____

_____

_____

_____

_____

_____

_____

_____

_____

_____

_____

SEPTEMBER

*O*ur lives are a mosaic
of little things,
like putting a rose in a
vase on the table.

INGRID TROBISCH

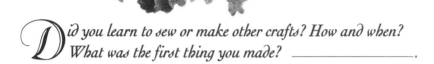

*D*id you learn to sew or make other crafts? How and when? What was the first thing you made? ————————.

*T*ell about a special outing you took with your mother or your father. _____

_____
_____
_____
_____
_____
_____
_____
_____
_____
_____
_____
_____
_____
_____
_____
_____
_____
_____
_____
_____
_____
_____

September

What was the most tender day in your childhood?

_____

_____

_____

_____

_____

_____

_____

_____

_____

_____

_____

_____

_____

_____

_____

_____

_____

_____

_____

_____

_____

_____

What was your favorite subject in grade school, junior high, and high school? What was your major in college? Why?

_____.
_____.
_____.
_____.
_____.
_____.
_____.
_____.
_____.
_____.
_____.
_____.
_____.
_____.
_____.
_____.
_____.
_____.
_____.
_____.
_____.
_____.
_____.

September

As a young person did you volunteer for work in church, community, or social services? Tell me about it. _____.

When did you move away from home? Describe where you lived and how you felt about it. _____

_____
_____
_____
_____
_____
_____
_____
_____
_____
_____
_____
_____
_____
_____
_____
_____
_____
_____
_____
_____
_____

September

*W*ho was your best friend after you were married? Describe some of the fun things you did together. _____.

_____
_____
_____
_____
_____
_____
_____
_____
_____
_____
_____
_____
_____
_____
_____
_____
_____
_____
_____
_____
_____
_____
_____

What are your spiritual strengths?

_____ .
_____ .
_____ .

September

How would you like to grow spiritually? _____

_____

What special talents did your parents nurture in you? How have you developed those talents? _____.

_____
_____
_____
_____
_____
_____
_____
_____
_____
_____
_____
_____
_____
_____
_____
_____
_____
_____
_____
_____
_____
_____

September

What would you like to learn to do? Why? _____.

_____

_____

_____

_____

_____

_____

_____

_____

_____

_____

_____

_____

_____

_____

_____

_____

_____

_____

_____

_____

_____

_____

*What would you
do differently in life
if you could?*

_____.
_____.
_____.
_____.
_____.
_____.
_____.
_____.
_____.
_____.
_____.
_____.
_____.
_____.
_____.
_____.
_____.
_____.
_____.
_____.
_____.
_____.
_____.
_____.
_____.
_____.

September

Describe your personal style in clothing, make up or skin care, and hair care:

• _____ •
• _____ •
• _____ •
• _____ •
• _____ •
• _____ •
• _____ •
• _____ •
• _____ •
• _____ •
• _____ •
• _____ •
• _____ •
• _____ •
• _____ •
• _____ •
• _____ •
• _____ •
• _____ •
• _____ •
• _____ •

OCTOBER

"How will our children
know who they are
if they don't know
where they came from?"

Ma in *Grapes of Wrath*

Who are some of the best speakers you have ever heard? Why? _____.

_____

_____

_____

_____

_____

_____

_____

_____

_____

_____

_____

_____

_____

_____

_____

_____

_____

_____

_____

_____

_____

_____

October

What spiritual legacy would you like to leave for others? Why is this important to you? _____.

_____
_____
_____
_____
_____
_____
_____
_____
_____
_____
_____
_____
_____
_____
_____
_____
_____
_____
_____
_____
_____
_____
_____

October

*T*ell about a canning or harvesting experience. _____

_____

_____

_____

_____

_____

_____

_____

_____

_____

_____

_____

_____

_____

_____

_____

_____

_____

_____

_____

_____

_____

_____

_____

_____

October

*What Bible verse or
Scripture puzzles you the
most? Which blesses you
the most? Why?*

_____.
_____.
_____.
_____.
_____.
_____.
_____.
_____.
_____.
_____.
_____.
_____.
_____.
_____.
_____.
_____.
_____.
_____.
_____.
_____.
_____.
_____.
_____.

October

Have you ever been in an accident, had surgery or a long illness? Tell me about it. _____.

_____
_____
_____
_____
_____
_____
_____
_____
_____
_____
_____
_____
_____
_____
_____
_____
_____
_____
_____
_____
_____
_____
_____
_____
_____

October

What responsibilities did your parents require of you as a child? Explain how this affected your growth and develpment.

_____

_____

_____

_____

_____

_____

_____

_____

_____

_____

_____

_____

_____

_____

_____

_____

_____

_____

_____

_____

_____

_____

_____

_____

October

*N*ame your favorite hobby. When and where did you start doing it? Why do you enjoy it? ———————————.

*When and where did
you buy your first house?
Describe the house and explain
any significance it held for you.*

_____.
_____.
_____.
_____.
_____.
_____.
_____.
_____.
_____.
_____.
_____.
_____.
_____.
_____.
_____.
_____.
_____.
_____.
_____.
_____.
_____.
_____.
_____.
_____.

October

W hat is the strangest thing you have ever seen? _____.

_____

_____

_____

_____

_____

_____

_____

_____

_____

_____

_____

_____

_____

_____

_____

_____

_____

_____

_____

_____

_____

*T*ell about a memorable hotel or resort you have visited. Describe the location and tell about experiences that were significant. —.

October

Did you ever go on a hayride or bob for apples? Tell about fun harvest activities you enjoyed with other young people.

*As a teenager,
did you belong to a club or
church youth group? Tell me about
the individuals in the group who
were most significant to you*

_____.

_____.

_____.

_____.

_____.

_____.

_____.

_____.

_____.

_____.

_____.

_____.

_____.

_____.

_____.

_____.

_____.

_____.

_____.

_____.

_____.

_____.

_____.

October

Share some helpful home remedies or tips for good health:

_____
_____
_____
_____
_____
_____
_____
_____
_____
_____
_____
_____
_____
_____
_____
_____
_____
_____
_____

NOVEMBER

In our family an experience
was not finished,
not truly experienced,
unless written down or
shared with another.

ANNE MORROW LINDBERGH

What individuals have had the greatest impact on your spiritual life? How did they impact your life? _____.

_____
_____
_____
_____
_____
_____
_____
_____
_____
_____
_____
_____
_____
_____
_____
_____
_____
_____
_____
_____
_____

What is your most treasured possession and why? _____.

What Bible character would you most like to meet? Why?

What is your most vivid memory of being pregnant?

November

How did you choose my name and why?

What is your most poignant memory about my childhood?

_____

_____

_____

_____

_____

_____

_____

_____

_____

_____

_____

_____

_____

_____

_____

_____

_____

_____

_____

_____

_____

November

What was a favorite Thanksgiving tradition in your family?

_____

_____
_____
_____
_____
_____
_____
_____
_____
_____
_____
_____
_____
_____
_____
_____
_____
_____
_____
_____
_____
_____
_____

*What are some things
from your childhood
that you are thankful for?*

_____.
_____.
_____.
_____.
_____.
_____.
_____.
_____.
_____.
_____.
_____.
_____.
_____.
_____.
_____.
_____.
_____.
_____.
_____.
_____.
_____.
_____.

November

What childhood memory first comes to mind when you think about winter? How do you respond to that memory?.

_____
_____
_____
_____
_____
_____
_____
_____
_____
_____
_____
_____
_____
_____
_____
_____
_____
_____
_____
_____
_____
_____
_____
_____

$\mathcal{W}$hat are your childhood memories of going to church or of interacting with other Christians? _____.

_____
_____
_____
_____
_____
_____
_____
_____
_____
_____
_____
_____
_____
_____
_____
_____
_____
_____
_____
_____
_____
_____
_____

*W*hat family custom would you like to pass on to your children and grandchildren? _____.

_____
_____
_____
_____
_____
_____
_____
_____
_____
_____
_____
_____
_____
_____
_____
_____
_____
_____
_____
_____
_____
_____
_____

*What new tradition would
you like to start in the family?
What is its significance?*

_____.

_____.

_____.

_____.

_____.

_____.

_____.

_____.

_____.

_____.

_____.

_____.

_____.

_____.

_____.

_____.

_____.

_____.

_____.

_____.

_____.

Share a favorite Thanksgiving or
Christmas recipe:

_____
_____
_____
_____
_____
_____
_____
_____
_____
_____
_____
_____
_____
_____
_____
_____
_____
_____
_____
_____
_____

DECEMBER

If everything special and warm
and happy in my formative years
could have been consolidated
into one word, that word
would have been *Christmas.*

GLORIA GAITHER

Tell about some Christmas rituals in your family and how you felt about them. _____.

_____
_____
_____
_____
_____
_____
_____
_____
_____
_____
_____
_____
_____
_____
_____
_____
_____
_____
_____
_____
_____
_____
_____

*W*ere you ever in a Christmas program? How did you respond to the experience? _____ .

_____
_____
_____
_____
_____
_____
_____
_____
_____
_____
_____
_____
_____
_____
_____
_____
_____
_____
_____
_____
_____
_____
_____

December

What favorite Christmas treasures have you kept from year to year? Share their origins. _____.

_____
_____
_____
_____
_____
_____
_____
_____
_____
_____
_____
_____
_____
_____
_____
_____
_____
_____
_____
_____
_____
_____
_____
_____

Tell about a memorable Christmas visit with relatives.

—————————————————— .
—————————————————— .
—————————————————— .
——————————————————————— .
——————————————————————— .
——————————————————————— .
——————————————————————— .
——————————————————————— .
——————————————————————— .
——————————————————————— .
——————————————————————— .
——————————————————————— .
——————————————————————— .
——————————————————————— .
——————————————————————— .
——————————————————————— .
——————————————————————— .
——————————————————————— .
——————————————————————— .
——————————————————————— .
——————————————————————— .

December

$\mathcal{W}$hat is your favorite Christmas carol? Why? _____.

_____
_____
_____
_____
_____
_____
_____
_____
_____
_____
_____
_____
_____
_____
_____
_____
_____
_____
_____
_____
_____
_____
_____
_____

*D*id you have a Christmas stocking as a child or a special ornament? What did it look like? _____.

_____
_____
_____
_____
_____
_____
_____
_____
_____
_____
_____
_____
_____
_____
_____
_____
_____
_____
_____
_____
_____
_____

December

*D*escribe the Christmas that has been the most meaningful to you.

_____

_____
_____
_____
_____
_____
_____
_____
_____
_____
_____
_____
_____
_____
_____
_____
_____
_____
_____
_____
_____
_____

What would be the most wonderful gift you could receive? Why?

_____
_____
_____
_____
_____
_____
_____
_____
_____
_____
_____
_____
_____
_____
_____
_____
_____
_____
_____
_____
_____
_____

December

Tell me about a time when God answered a specific prayer for you.

What would you like to see happen in the next ten years?

_____.

_____.
_____.
_____.
_____.
_____.
_____.
_____.
_____.
_____.
_____.
_____.
_____.
_____.
_____.
_____.
_____.
_____.
_____.
_____.
_____.
_____.

What has been the happiest time of your life?

*What word best describes
your life? Explain why.*

_____ .
_____ .
_____ .
_____ .
_____ .
_____ .
_____ .
_____ .
_____ .
_____ .
_____ .
_____ .
_____ .
_____ .
_____ .
_____ .
_____ .
_____ .
_____ .
_____ .
_____ .
_____ .
_____ .
_____ .
_____ .

December

What advice about life do you want others to remember?

_____
_____
_____
_____
_____
_____
_____
_____
_____
_____
_____
_____
_____
_____
_____
_____
_____
_____
_____

Notes

_____

_____

_____

_____

_____

_____

_____

_____

_____

_____

_____

_____

_____

_____

_____

_____

_____

_____

Notes

_____
_____
_____
_____
_____
_____
_____
_____
_____
_____
_____
_____
_____
_____
_____
_____
_____
_____
_____

Notes

_____
_____
_____
_____
_____
_____
_____
_____
_____
_____
_____
_____
_____
_____
_____
_____
_____
_____
_____

Photos

Photos

Photos

Photos